FORMULA ONE

David Clayton

CLASH

by ticktock

Copyright © ticktock Entertainment Ltd 2008

First published in Great Britain in 2008 by ticktock Media Ltd,
2 Orchard Business Centre, North Farm Road, Tunbridge Wells, Kent, TN2 3XF

project editor and picture researcher: Ruth Owen
ticktock project designer: Sara Greasley

With thanks to series editors Honor Head and Jean Coppendale.

Thank you to Lorraine Petersen and the members of nasen

ISBN 978 1 84696 721 4 pbk

Printed in China

Picture credits (t=top; b=bottom; c=centre; l=left; r=right):

Anglia Press Agency/Rex Features: 29t. David Bebber/Reuters/Corbis: 31. Bettmann/Corbis: 10. Gero
Breloer/epa/Corbis: OFC. Jens Buettner/epa/Corbis: 27b. Getty Images: 4t. Alex Grimm/Reuters/Corbis: 5t. Mike
Hayward/Alamy: 9t. Don Heiny/Corbis: 9b. Kolvenbach/Alamy: 19. Bob Masters Classic Car Images/Alamy: 6.
Christopher Morris/Corbis: 20. Kerim Okten/epa/Corbis: 4-5. pbpgalleries/Alamy: 8. Popperfoto/Getty Images: 6-7.
Reuters/Corbis: 24-25. Rex Features: 26, 29b. Schlegelmilch/Corbis: 14, 21, 22-23, 27t, 28b. Shutterstock: 1, 2-3. 11b,
18. Silverstone Circuits Limited: 15. Sipa Press/Rex Features: 12-13, 28t. ticktock Media Archive 11t.

Every effort has been made to trace copyright holders, and we apologise in advance for any omissions. We would be
pleased to insert the appropriate acknowledgments in any subsequent edition of this publication.

Contents

CHAPTER 1

WHAT IS FORMULA ONE?

SPEED!

2007 – Ferrari driver Kimi Raikkonen makes the fastest lap of the season. His average speed was 215.89 km/h.

CRASHES!

2006 – Mayhem at Indianapolis, USA! Ten cars went out of the race, but no one was hurt.

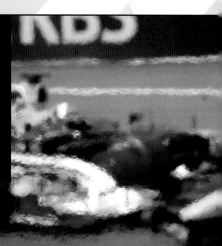

Formula One is the World Championship of the International Automobile Federation. Races, called grand prix, take place every year in different countries around the world.

STARS!

2006 – Michael Schumacher retires. He won 91 races and was World Champion seven times.

CHAPTER 2

THE BIRTH OF SPEED

Fast cars are not new. Cars made by the French company Bugatti were doing over 200 km/h in grand prix races 80 years ago!

The 2/2.5 litre "Bugatti 35" won over 1,000 races during the period 1924 to 1931.

Grand prix races were often held on normal roads not specially made tracks.

As a result of this, many drivers and spectators were killed.

Races lasted for 10 hours or more. Two drivers would take turns to drive each car.

In 1950, the Formula One World Championship started with seven races.

Cars made by the Italian company Alfa Romeo won six of the races.

The Alfa Romeos had a top speed of about 313 km/h.

1951 – Italian driver Giuseppe "Nino" Farina wins a race in an Alfa Romeo.

In the 1960s, new models of cars joined Formula One.

Cars made by Lotus won 12 championships in 12 years. These cars cut through the air like bullets!

Lotus cars were light, low and fast!

The engine was behind the driver.

The driver lay back in the seat.

The petrol was in tanks on either side of the driver's seat.

1962 – Lotus-Climax 25

CARS WENT FROM THIS...

1968 – Lotus 49B

...TO THIS...

1978 – Lotus 79

...TO THIS!

CHAPTER 3

FORMULA ONE SAFETY

The new Formula One cars were fast, but they were not safe. There was little protection for the driver if they hit something.

In 1968, the World Champion Jim Clark was killed. His car skidded, turned over and hit a tree.

Jim Clark in 1964. He won 25 grand prix races in his career.

Today, cars have "crumple zones" and a tough inner "shell" wrapped around the driver.

Race circuits also have better crash barriers.

Another safety problem with Formula One cars is worn tyres which do not grip the road.

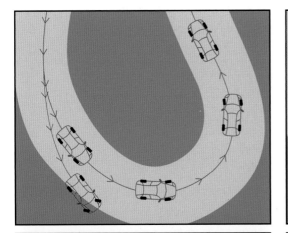

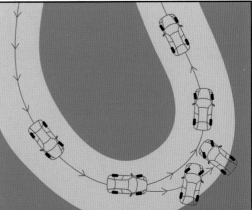

If your front tyres wear, your car goes straight on when you try to turn.

If your back tyres wear, your car slides if you try to turn.

Parts called wings were added to Formula One cars. Wings on a plane help to lift the plane up. Formula One car wings are designed to force the car down. This gives the tyres more grip.

Rear wing

Did this solve all of the drivers' safety problems? No.

Front wing

Brazilian driver Ayrton Senna was World Champion three times. In 1994, he was killed during the San Marino Grand Prix at Imola, Italy.

Senna lost control of his car and hit a concrete wall at almost 320 km/h.

"When Senna died, I was nine and he was my hero. I cried, but he showed me that you've got to make the most of your life."
Driver Lewis Hamilton

Today, circuits have sprung Armco barriers and tyres around the edge. The barriers and tyres absorb the shock of a crash.

Medical services are also spread out around the circuit. This means they can get to an accident faster.

CHAPTER 4

CIRCUITS

Formula One grands prix are held on specially built circuits and on circuits that include normal roads.

Formula One circuits all have fast sections and left and right-hand bends. The Eau Rouge corner at Spa has all these things in one place!

Spa-Francochamps circuit, Belgium

Eau Rouge corner

Drivers take Eau Rouge at over 300 km/h.

Spa is the longest circuit at 6.97 kilometres.

Spa is such a big circuit it can be sunny on one side and raining on the other. This can cause problems.

Formula One cars have dry track tyres and wet track tyres. At Spa, a driver might be using dry track tyres and suddenly reach a wet section of track.

Hangar Straight is the fastest point at 290 km/h.

Silverstone circuit, UK

Brooklands is the slowest point at 95 km/h.

The Silverstone circuit in the UK was once an airfield. It is one of the fastest grand prix circuits because it only has a few tight corners. It is 5.1 kilometres long.

The most famous grand prix circuit is Monaco. The track zig-zags around the city's streets.

Monaco is narrow with many tight turns. The wall, crash barriers and other cars are always close.

It is very easy to make a mistake!

Monaco is the shortest circuit at 3.34 kilometres.

> **"Monaco is like riding a bicycle around your living room..."**
>
> Driver Nelson Piquet

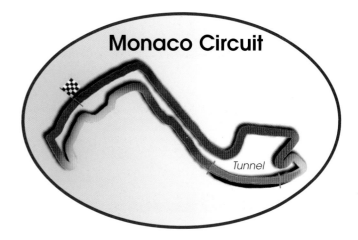

Monaco Circuit

Tunnel

At Monaco, the race goes through a tunnel. It's the circuit's only fast section.

CHAPTER 5

FORMULA ONE CARS

The red Ferrari is probably the most famous racing car in the world.

Many cars have been as fast or faster than the Ferrari, but everybody knows the famous name and badge.

Ferrari badge

Ferrari won the Formula One World Constructors' Championship six years running from 1999 to 2004. They also won it in 2007.

At the end of the 2007 season, Ferrari had won 201 Grand Prix races.

In 2007, the McLaren team launched the new MP4-22. They were leading the 2007 Constructors' Championship. However, they were disqualified for spying on Ferrari's car designs.

2007 – testing the MP4-22

MCLAREN MP4-22

- 2.4 litre engine/ 780 Bhp
- 20,000 revs per minute
- 0 to 160 km/h in 3.4 seconds
- Stops in just over 3 seconds at 300 km/h

CHAPTER 6

THE RACE

Before the race, the driver and the crew talk tactics. They decide when to make pit stops for fuel, and which tyres to use.

During practice laps, the driver and the car's onboard computers give the crew feedback.

Lewis Hamilton watches a video of a practice lap.

The crew spend hours making adjustments to the car.

The driver must also plan his race. He plans which line to take on each corner and when to brake.

On the Saturday of a grand prix weekend, the drivers drive in qualifying laps.

The drivers who complete the fastest qualifying laps get the best starting positions on the grid.

Mechanic

Sunday is race day.

After final checks, the mechanics push the cars to their grid positions.

The grid

The start of the race is close.

The drivers start their engines.

Away they go on the warm-up lap. They zig-zag their wheels to get the tyres sticky.

Then they're back on the grid.

The front place on the grid is called "pole position".

Five red lights go on, one at a time.

ONE, TWO, THREE, FOUR, FIVE.

Then the lights go out altogether.

VROOOM! THEY'RE AWAY!

They are off!

The drivers must watch
out for stalled cars.

They must focus.

Remember their race plan.

Don't get carried away on the
first bend and run into trouble.

DON'T END UP LIKE THIS!

2001 – Brazilian driver Luciano Burti crashes at the first corner of the German Grand Prix at Hockenheim. He was OK!

During the race, the driver makes pit stops.
In less than nine seconds, the crew will refuel
the car and change all four tyres.

The lollipop man shows the driver
where to stop, and when to go.

Refueller

Rear tyre fitter

Rear jack man

The team manager is in contact with the driver at all times through his headphones.

The engine's performance is shown on computer screens in the pits.

If everything goes to plan, the driver gets the chequered flag and wins the race!

CHAPTER 7

DRIVERS

MICHAEL SCHUMACHER

Michael Schumacher is the most successful Formula One driver of all time.

He had 91 grand prix wins – 13 in one season!

Schumacher was aggressive and daring in the dry. In the rain, he was brilliant.

2006 – winning the French Grand Prix.

2000 – winning the European Grand Prix in rain.

Fans called him "The Rain King". He drove 30 races in the rain and won 17 of them.

LEWIS HAMILTON

Lewis Hamilton started kart racing aged 6 years. He became European Karting Champion in 2000.

Hamilton wins his first race aged 8 years.

Winning the British Grand Prix in 2008.

Hamilton drove his first Formula One grand prix in 2007. He was just 22. In 2007, he came second in the Drivers' Championship – he missed the top spot by just one point!

"Racing is instinct. You can't teach it. I saw the chance of success in my first two races, got stuck in and came out on top."

Lewis Hamilton

NEED TO KNOW WORDS

aggressive (driving) Driving that takes chances.

biofuel Fuels that are made from plant matter instead of oil.

circuit A track that starts and finishes in the same place.

crew The people who prepare the car and the driver for the race.

crumple zone The outer part of a car that gives way to absorb the shock of a crash.

Formula One World Constructors' title The prize given to the car makers with the most points at the end of the season.

grand prix race A Formula One race that is part of the World Championship.

grid The starting positions of the cars before the race begins.

instinct The ability to do things without being told or shown.

International Automobile Federation The international organisation that runs most motorsport.

lap Once around a circuit.

lollipop man The member of the pit crew who uses a sign, like a big lollipop, to tell the driver where to stop. He keeps the driver in place until the car is ready to go.

mayhem Extreme trouble.

pit stop When a car comes into its team's "pit" or garage area, usually to add fuel or change tyres.

pole position The front position on the grid as the fastest qualifier.

qualifying Time trials that take place the day before the race. They decide the starting positions on the grid – fastest at the front, slowest at the back.

retire To give up racing, or to fail to finish a race.

season The period of time during which a series of races are held.

sprung Armco barriers Steel barriers around a circuit that absorb the force of a crash.

sticky (tyres) When the tyres have softened and warmed up so they grip the track better.

INTO THE FUTURE

What does the future hold for Formula One?

- Some people are worried that Formula One is not "green" enough in today's world. Engines are being developed which run partly on biofuels. These fuels are made from plants and will be better for the environment.

- Safety is still a big issue. Some fans say Formula One is now so safe it's not exciting enough. The famous English driver Stirling Moss said the danger was why he wanted to drive. Other people remember drivers, such as Ayrton Senna, who were killed. What do you think?

- Fans would like to have more races in cities. Perhaps the streets of London will be used as a circuit!

2004 – Formula One cars take part in a parade to show how London's streets could be used as a circuit.

FORMULA ONE ONLINE

Websites

http://www.formula1.com/
The official Formula One website

http://www.lewishamilton.com/
The official Lewis Hamilton website

http://www.autosport.com/
The website of the leading Formula One motor magazine

INDEX